# Perfectly

# IMP∃RFECT

A Collection of Words and Thoughts

Volume III

# Perfectly

# IMPƎRFECT

A Collection of Words and Thoughts

Volume III

## Amber Whitted

Chicago

PERFECTLY IMPERFECT: A COLLECTION OF WORDS AND
THOUGHTS VOLUME 3

www.amberwhitted.com

Back cover photo credit: Karen London (LondonKay)
Cover artwork: Creative Blessings by Jelaine Bell, © 2018
Website: www.creativeblessingsdesign.com

Library of Congress Cataloging-in-Publication Data

Whitted, Amber, 1981 –
 – 1st ed  p.cm
 ISBN-13: 978-0692107041
 ISBN-10: 0692107045
   1.   Poetry   2.   Poetry – African American   3.   African American
        Literature   I.   Title


First edition: July 2018


10 9 8 7 6 5 4 3 2 1

We write words

to capture the moments

that we dare not let go.


AMW

# Table of Contents

Defining the paradox… (An Introduction)

## I.  I live and dream in color…

## II.  Love is the ink…

## III.   Everything about her...

## IV.  Five Seven Five...

## V.  These are the conversations...

## VI.  …God gave me wings to fly

# Defining the paradox...

An introduction

*Let the words of my mouth and the meditation of my heart be acceptable in your sight, O LORD, my rock and my redeemer. (Psalm 19:14)*

Thank you, Father, for allowing me to have the gift of words and the chance to share them. I am grateful and humbled that You have chosen me. All glory and praise belong to You.

The title **Perfectly Imperfect**, was originally a play on my birthday (July 6th). I made the joke a while back that I was born in the perfect month (7) on the imperfect day (6), which should explain a lot of my behavior. Using those numbers as the inspiration for the title made sense. As I began to write this book, it began to mean so much more.

A friend asked me if I have ever broken down on stage while reciting a poem. There were many times where I could feel the tears as I spoke; however, I was able to hold it in. Fear of being vulnerable will do that to you.

Truthfully, I have always felt the need to be viewed as perfect. I am not sure if it was due to the pressure of being the older sibling, growing up as a church girl, or just the general highs and lows that come with maturity. Regardless of the reason, I put that yoke on my shoulders as if I owed the world something. Every time I failed, the yoke got heavier. I managed to keep a smile on my face, but that was because I felt it was expected of me. Yes, even when it hurt.

As humans, we will never be perfect. There will always flaws, but that is what makes us uniquely beautiful. Accepting my perfect imperfections has allowed me to release those fears. It was a chance for me to finally say, 'Here I am, flaws and all. No use in being perceived as perfect, especially since all of you are just as crazy as I am!'

It is my hope that you will see your perfectly imperfect self in these pages and be blessed by each word.

There are so many people that I need to thank for making me the woman and writer that I am. I would run out of pages if I listed them all. Or, I could try to shorten the list, but I would end up leaving off someone and that would be the *worst!* So, I will simply say this:

To all of those that I hold closest to my heart: by blood or by bond, current or past, mentor or mentee. These words are for you. I know the love that you have for me will always be there. As long as I have breath, I will do all that I can to show you how much I love you too.

No, I'm not perfect.
Still, one thing I know is true –
my heart's full of love.

# Perfectly
# IMPΞRFECT

A Collection of Words and Thoughts

Volume III

# I

I live and dream in color.
Rich shades of mahogany
bond with struggle and progress
in native tapestry.

# Identity

Each day, you wake up.
You fix your hair.
You put on perfect makeup
with heels and pearls,
jeans, t-shirts,
or boho dresses.
But my guess is
that's not who you really are.
Show me who you really are.

Each morning you stand up,
stretch your legs,
and prepare to man up.
You hit the block or wall street.
You're grand, yet
something tells me
that's not who you really are.
Show me who you really are.

The you before disappointment took hold
and you forgot everything you know.

Every night, you come home.
You fix a meal to be eaten alone.
You get upset
'cuz no one's called your phone.
But you don't call them either.
Is that who you really are?
Show them who you really are.

Each evening, you rush in.
You barely eat
but get the babies tucked in.
You've got no time left
for kisses and loving
from the one who should see
who you really are.
Show them who you really are.

The you before you lost identity
and everyone told you who you should be.

Show us who you are.
The world is waiting
for you manifest your light.
Since everyone else is taken,
you might as well drop your mask.
Release your past.
You rarely get a second chance,
Take it.
Show us who you are.
Show us who you really are.

# Literary Artistry

I want to paint a picture with my words.
Strokes of light and dark
paint layers through penned prose.
I want you to see the roads I've walked,
captured and filled with emotion
through verbal release.

I want to compose a symphony with my words.
Quarter and half notes
make whole the fragments of unfinished rhyme.
I want the melody to ring through time
and kiss your ears sweetly
through the form of poetry.

I want to dance for you through my words.
A delicate balance of certainty and fear
courageously moves through the moment
to pull you near.
And should you choose,
dance with me in literary harmony.
My stanza will follow as you lead.

I want you to see my artistry.
Song for scribe,
portrait for pen,
lyric to movement
and return again
to the place where
it all began —
words.

# The Heart Knows The Way

The sands of time become wet concrete
when it's time to walk.
Each step taken
becomes permanently etched,
and those you've never met
will know that someone was there.
Newness fills the lungs
as oxygen becomes memory.
When the mind fails,
the soul always remembers
and sparks the embers
that feed the senses needed to return.
Glory days.
Mistakes made.
All lessons learned.
Life always leaves a mark
long after time has passed.
Feet may never walk the path again,
but the heart will always know the way.

# Restraint

I want to put pen to paper
to release my thoughts
of you,
but everything about you
makes me want to curse.

So that's the end of this verse.

# Sankofa

Echoes of your influence linger.
Still,
I take only what I need
to journey on.
Promise beckons me forward,
and closed time offers
nothing new.

# We Be (Sometimes)

We be loud sometimes.
Vocals over tight beats.
Loud colors.
Loud streets.
Sirens signaling somber soliloquies
that you don't be hearing.
We still be loud
sometimes.

We be extra sometimes.
Big bragging.
Tongue wagging.
Story swapping to stay
the most envied one in the room.
They don't always be true,
'cuz we be extra
sometimes.

We be scared sometimes.
Masking fears and tears.
Full of pride,
we keep it inside.
Maybe if we weren't targets,
we could show our heart a bit.
We just be scared
sometimes.

Truth be told,
the world be unprepared
for what we really be.
We be beautiful.

We be wise.
We be innovative.
But in their eyes,
stereotypes be
too good to let go.

And we?
We be trendsetting
and keeping our greatness
on the low.
When you ain't looking,
we be letting it show.
But we know you be seeing
sometimes.

# Chill

a Saturday morning type thing

I have no plans today.
I just want to sleep
until the natural sunlight
opens my eyes.
Even then,
I'll stay in my bed and stretch.
I'll let the morning sun
kiss my curves
and realize that I am thankful
to be alive.
I'll have cake and tea for breakfast
if I choose.
I know that I have weight to lose,
but this moment is about me.
I will applaud my informality.
This day of rest was needed
both physically and spiritually.
Nope.
No plans today.
Just relaxation and freedom
to do whatever I want,
like write a poem
or two
or three.

# King

He stands.
He is a perfect dichotomy
of patience and pressure,
of peace and pain,
of readiness and raw ability.
No longer waiting
for permission to be,
he's got a destiny to reach
and a legacy to leave.
They don't see your beauty
like I do.
Generations will prosper
because you walked in truth.
I will gladly submit
just to be where you are.
You lead in love
with a servant's heart.
You protect me as your priority
and make my dreams your reality.
You are more than a man.
You are royalty.
I call you king.

# Perfectly Imperfect

I am perfectly imperfect
and elegantly errored.
I am a being in development,
healing from her past
and moving toward her future
through a comically peculiar present.
I am not where I could be,
yet it is by grace that I'm not
where I should be.
What I lack is coming quickly
in Kairos time.
Daily, I am learning what is in my heart
as time reveals a masterpiece.
My reality is not your ideology
nor will you hinder my release.
I will not apologize for my feelings.
I will not apologize for my flaws.
I will not apologize for the very things
that cause others to admire and pause.
I am merely the shell
for a spirit that will live eternally.
I'm passing through to share my gifts,
spread love and speak life.
I am humbly here to bring light
and encourage those
who are perfectly imperfect
just like me.

# II

Love is the ink
that fills the pages
of our life stories.

# In All Honesty

I still write about you sometimes.
Sweet sonnets relive moments
of us at our best.
We were love undefined,
captured in time with lyrics
penned by another
before I could capture you.
And every time those notes
ring through my ears,
I hear you whisper,
"Yes, I remember too."

Somehow,
I don't think that I'm imagining things.

# Slow Jams

We were about 15 deep that night.
Clowning,
laughing,
having a good time.

And you were there.
And I was there.

Then someone brought a radio
and the music began to play.
Soft music.
Slow music.
Slow jams.

And I listened
as it took me away.

I listened
to Maxwell,
to the Isley's,
to artists who took your mood
and made it mellow,
calm,
and cool.

And from across the room,
your eyes looked at me.

And I saw.

# Catch Me

an acrostic

I'm running
far from your embrace.
Yesterday we were platonic,
open only to imagination and
understanding that lines won't be
crossed.
All hope is lost
now that I've kissed you.

# Forbidden Fruit

Consider my life to be the garden of Eden,
and I am the garden's Eve.
Your game is a serpent to trick me
into learning to love and believe.
You say you'd hide no secret from me,
and I can rely on you.
I'm the Eve of my garden
and you're the forbidden fruit.

You're a portrait of perfect seduction
but no good at the core.
You kill my heart with every bite,
yet I still long for more.
You're trustworthy on the outside
and rotten at the root.
I'm the Eve of my garden
and you're the forbidden fruit.

# A Response To Love

Love,
it's not that I don't believe in you.
Please don't take my hesitancy as proof
that I am no longer willing to bear all.
Those who carried your moniker
have sometimes let the banner fall
and I have been bruised.

Love,
I wish I could see you with a child's eye.
I want to be innocent enough
to give freely the best of me
without fear of lack of reciprocity.
I know you got me.
This callous mind is not me.
For one moment,
I'll speak freely
with hopes that I don't have to
retreat into my shell.

Love,
I want you to hold me
with the warmth of the sun.
Gently kiss away
the tears that I refused to release.
I want you to bring me peace.
You said that you and time
can mend broken hearts.
As I start shedding
the garment of resentment,
fill in the missing parts

and cover the places that I lack.
Honestly,
I want the trusting spirit back.

Love,
I don't expect you to do all the work.
As you ease my fears,
I'll be willingly transparent.
I'll give you a clear view of all of me -
good,
bad,
and ugly.
Somehow, you'll still love me.
And I know you won't hurt me,
at least not intentionally.
Growing pains
will stretch and strain.
I know that your heart is pure,
so I'll endure just so I can keep saying
your name.

Love,
find me and I promise to give the same.
I can't promise to be perfect,
but I promise that I'm worth it.
What I don't know,
I'll learn along the way
if the pathway leads me to you.
Love.

# Broken Pottery

a reflection of us

I've got questions.
My life is lived in borrowed time
while my needs and mind
get left at honorable mention.
You told me,
"Slow down
and see what's in front of you.
I want all or none of you.
If you run too fast,
I can only catch some of you."
I wish you could see
from my point of view.
I see a future
where purpose propels purchase.
You'd know the fight was worth it.
But I don't want to fight alone.
I'd rather submit to your lead
as you follow the King
and we build a legacy.
My eyes want to see
your vision come into fruition
as a reward for how you've grown.
Too bad I didn't see this
until I was on my own.
Now we're staring at pieces
of broken pottery,
able to be repaired in skill hands
if we can withstand the pressure.
I get scared thinking of the work

beyond measure.
Does this jar of clay
still hold the Master's treasure?
I can't keep running.
You can't be complacent.
The plan must be adjacent
to a Higher calling.
No more pride.
No more stalling.
Still,
I've got questions.

# Tell Me Show Me

Tell me.
Show me.
Get to know me
and all of the deep
and wonderful things
about me.
Make me
a priority.
Let my femininity
surround your being.
Love me.
Like me.
Let your spirit invite me
to a place where I feel
lovely
and can return emotions
given to me.
Make me
easily
see the need that you have
for me.
Let your actions be
the backbone
of the words you speak.
Give me
a reason to believe
that the we are a necessity
and my being
as one entity
shouldn't be all that I see.
So,

Tell me.
Show me.
Get to know me.
Let your presence
grow on me.
And if I decide
to bless thee,
come become one with me.
Love me.
Like me.
Let your spirit invite me.
Make me
easily
see the need that you have
for me.
And maybe,
just maybe,
we
can
be.

# Easy

unspoken words between the sexes

I've heard it all too often.
Tell me,
is it easier?
Is it easier to lay your burdens
on my chest?
Knowing that I am your
sacred place to release stress,
here is where all your fears
simply rest.
Yet, what is kept in confidence
quickly becomes public knowledge.
I do the best that I can do
to walk through death
just to birth your nations.
My motivation is to ensure
that your bloodline continues.
But that's not good enough for you,
is it?
You're so quick to pull the rhetoric
that us sistas don't get it
and everything wrong in your life
is because we are the cause of it.
Pause for a bit.
Tell me,
is it easier?
I understand that for a man
born with rich melanin
life can be harder.
I know that you struggle

to raise your sons and daughters.
But why call us a queen
to get the kingdom
if you don't want to be bothered?
Is it easier to say
that my hair is too nappy?
Are my emotions too sappy?
Do I act too strong?
Is my weave too long?
Am I too thin?
Too fat?
Is my butt too flat?
Tell me,
do I nag too much?
Do I not provide the right touch?
Do I fail to keep my feelings
under control?
Am I too bourgeois
and not enough soul?
Am I too hood
and without class?
Do I play it too cool
and men like you pass?
Do I talk too much?
Do I bring too much drama?
Tell me,
do you say these things about your mama
to her face
where she can hear you clearly?
Recognize it or not,
some woman who loves you dearly
has the very qualities
that you find appalling.
Stop stalling.

Tell me,
is it easier?
We are told to suck it up,
accept our bad choices,
put on our big girl panties
and deal.
Let's be real,
we already know there is room
for improvement.
We're not perfect.
Far from it.
We're human.
Add to that the years
of misfortune and pain
often felt alongside of you,
in the absence of you,
and by you.
You have no clue
what we've been through.
Still,
no one will love you the way that I do.
No matter how you hurt me,
these tears still find a way
to make room for you.
So why do you blame me
for your ills?
I promise,
if you just own it,
I will love you still.
But I guess it's just easier.

# Soul Tie

a kyrielle poem

I cleaned my room out yesterday;
found plenty things to throw away.
Still, one thing lingers; sad, but true –
I can't seem to get rid of you.

I changed my hair, revamped my style,
and bought new shoes to make me smile.
But despite all that's fresh and new,
I can't seem to get rid of you.

I took a trip across the sea.
I penned my thoughts in poetry.
Yet, one thing remains when I'm through –
I can't seem to get rid of you.

Despite the purging, prayers and tears,
your memory still lingers here.
I guess I must accept the truth –
I can't seem to get rid of you.

# Next Lifetime

for love that was never meant to happen

I met you in my first life,
down by the banks of the Nile.
You were a prince,
an heir to the throne;
I was a poor peasant child.
Despite my appearance
disheveled and wild,
you saw the beauty in me.
You taught me about your trips
around the world.
I taught you about love and poetry.
But it wasn't meant to be.
Royals and peasants do not mix.
Despite your pleas to your father,
that was something you could not fix.
 As African violets bloomed
on the walls of the palace divine,
you married a princess
and I cried, "Next lifetime."

We met again in a foreign land
called Georgia.
This time, I was your wife.
We jumped the broom,
you impregnated my womb,
and I promised you
the best of my life.
It would hurt me at night
to see you come home

beaten and abused,
so I made that one room shack
feel like the palace
that my king was used to.
But who knew that our master's obsession
would become so defiled.
To cover his tracks,
he killed both me and our unborn child.
They sold you off to Tennessee.
For rebellion, they blacked out your eyes.
Every morning you'd cry out in the fields,
"Next lifetime."

Then you were a smooth trumpet player
from up Harlem's way.
You could charm any woman
with any note you'd play.
But every dog has his day,
because you never would've guessed
that a quiet preacher's daughter
would know how to scat like that.
Every riff that you played,
I would match you note for note.
What we artistically displayed
was deeper than anything
that Hurston and Hughes ever wrote.
But my daddy said you were a waste of time.
Despite my feeble cries,
I married some old deacon
and you played 'Next Lifetime'.

We met many more times;
only a few I can remember:
Two leaves that fell from the same tree.

Two snowflakes in the cold of December.
Two raindrops that fell in the same sea
but managed to part in different directions.
Two lilies that grew on a warrior's tomb
to offer his widow comfort and affection.

And here you come again in my direction.

Still handsome, still fine.
Every word spoken stirs nostalgia
while every touch feels like the first time.
Still, you are hers
and I am his.
As much as we wish to change things,
it simply is what it is.
So, gently kiss my forehead
to stay on my mind.
And maybe,
just maybe,
we'll be butterflies in our next lifetime.

# III

Everything about her
defies and defines beauty.

# Invisible Life

Let's get the obvious out of the way.

I'm short and full-figured
without many of the assets
that distinguish a Black female.
I'm slightly rhythm deficient
with a plethora of awkward tales.
Though I try to allow
positivity to prevail,
sometimes
my slightly crooked smile
goes stale
and I fail.
Occasionally, I blend in.
Though I always play to win,
I refuse to do so
if my character must spin.
Bed for baubles
has never been my game of choice.
I have a distinctive voice.
Though not full of riffs,
I sing from the soul.
I give all of me,
even when it is not required.
That generosity hurts me
when I find that my services
are no longer desired.
That leads me to believe
that I am leading an invisible life.
I'm too wholesome
to be a ho,

but not whole enough
to be a wife.
And for any attention that I seek,
I must fight.

Well, that's fine.
I don't mind getting dirty
if it means
keeping my past buried.
Try as you might,
you will never limit my greatness.
My Creator made me limitless.
He infused favor
in my DNA
and skillfully allowed
the double helixes
to push through my cranium
for my wisdom to display.
Yeah,
that's why my hair
looks this way.
My skin is kissed with melanin
and coated in caramel,
which pays homage
to my roots overseas.
Natural and spiritual beauty
is why I still haunt
your man's dreams.
Still, you say I'm living
an invisible life.
I'm not fine enough
for forever,
but I'm too respectful
for just one night.

I'd be upset,
but I'm too busy shining bright.

Don't mind me.
I'm just
skating through your mental
with my superwoman cape on,
wittingly wording
my weakness willingly
if that is what
will make you strong.
I know it's not about me.
A queen leads her subjects
by example;
that's why they praise her faithfully.
For her king,
she'll go to war wisely
but be soft enough
to let him lead.
Her heart beats like a warrior,
For her family, she'll bleed.
And that's me.
No need for a standing ovation;
I got your attention
as I walked through the door.
No extra skin showing,
but your jaw hit the floor.

What's more,
I speak with the authority given
by God Himself.
I require the approval,
appraisal,
or acknowledgement

of no one else.
I speak life in lyrical rhythm
that it touches the soul,
using class as a filter
and maintaining self-control
simply because I choose to.
No need to
eloquently unleash vernacular.
I use vast vocabulary
to keep my verses virtuous.
Still,
don't let the smooth taste fool you.
This diamond has been
polished by my Creator.
I am able to withstand
every negative nomenclature.
I speak the truth in love,
straight
with no chaser.

So, it's impossible to say
that I'm leading an invisible life.
I'm married to my purpose
with the singular focus
to live the way that I'd like.
And what's nice
is I ain't even begun
to take flight.
Just sit tight.
Alright?

# Human

She gives birth to nations and lands.
She heals diseases with the touch of her hands.
Her prayers move mountains and part the seas.
Her ears stay open to the weakest pleas.
Sometimes her needs fail to be met;
still, she serves humbly with no regret.
Her smile cures doubt until there's no trace.
There's nowhere warmer than her embrace.
She makes magic and gives hope
where there is none.
She opens her heart and give her all
to anyone.
She's a flowing well;
but when all is said and done,
when does she get to be human?

She nurtures children that aren't her own.
Even with little, she makes a house a home.
Her wisdom is learned from generations past
seasoned with lessons that she learned last.
Her children rise and call her blessed.
She remains calm when she is stressed.
Her love gives the courage to try,
but no one is there to see her cry.
Without help, she stands tall for society,
never once requesting reciprocity.
She doesn't realize
the right she's been robbed to see.
When does she get to be human?

You call her crazy.
You say she's mad.
You don't know her story
or the victories she's had.
You say she's bitter,
broken,
and scarred.
Who is the one that will heal her heart?
Who will love her and keep her warm?
Who covers the shelter in the storm?
She doesn't want to be strong all the time,
but who will be there to simply remind her
that she is human?

When does she get to be human?

# Indigo

She dyed her hair blue,
but not because she was sad.
It was because she heard
that he loved indigo.
She knew the shade was closer
to purple,
but she wasn't ready
to feel that deeply.
Not yet.
But her bet was that
he'd see the midnight hues
kissed with aqua
and flecks of denim and jade.
He'd want to know her name
and why she chose that shade.
Her well-played introduction
will spark a conversation
about love,
food,
and the things she believes in.
He'd open his heart
to breathe her in.
He'd appreciate the jewel
that she is –
a sapphire of the purest kind.
In his mind,
her beauty only comes second
to the diamond
that he left behind
for this chance meeting.
To him,

this conversation was no more
than an elongated greeting.
To her,
hopes of being seen
was the reason
that her heart was beating.
But she'll be alright.
She dyed her hair blue,
but not because she was sad.
It was because she heard
that he loved indigo.
It will be a different shade tomorrow.

# The Rebuttal

from the fat girl in the cookie aisle

To the gentleman who took time
from his busy schedule
to tell me how horribly unattractive I am...

After hearing your unsolicited complaints,
I get it.
I truly do.
You want someone unattainable,
jealousy-inducing,
and perfect.
Kind of like you think that you are.
By far, you have the right
to pursue what you choose.

You'll probably meet her at a gala.
She'll walk past you
in a perfectly fitted dress.
Classy enough to be given wife status
but sexy enough
to show a hint of her breasts.
My guess is that it'll be black.
Next to nothing at all,
that is your favorite thing to see
on our melanin.
Without hesitation,
you'll walk up to her
and begin a conversation
about your favorite subject:
yourself.

You'll proudly lay out
your 5-year plan to get wealth.
You'll lie about contacts you've made.
You'll exaggerate your accolades.
And once you've strutted
your feathers on parade,
you'll finally ask her,
"So, what do I need to know about you?"
As if on cue,
she'll respond in a sweet voice,
"I just want to take care of my husband,
his home,
and his goals."
Just like that you'll be sold.
Your singleness will go
on temporary hold
because this business merger
will be worth
putting on that band of gold.

What is really in your soul?

But pay me no never mind.
I'm just the fat girl in the cookie aisle
who's jealous that she'll never be that fine.

Your peers will congratulate you
on your selection of a fine wife.
This is the kind of respect
you've been waiting for all your life.
Even management is willing
to discuss your upward mobility;
that kind of promotion
makes your game flow easily.

New levels bring new devils.
Self-control is not in your nature.
If a woman is offering,
you feel obligated to take her.
So when you slip up
and leave something 'extra'
for your wife to find,
she'll come to you
with tears in her eyes and say,
"Baby, that's fine.
Just keep me safe
and bring home a check.
I will stay in line."
In no time,
she'll produce an heir to your throne.
True, you never wanted to be a father,
but it did feel good
to hear a child's voice in your home.
However, they need to stay well-behaved,
and your wife's body must stay tight.
'Cuz nothing should ruin your perfect life.

Are your motives right?

But don't listen to me.
I'm just the fat girl in the cookie aisle
speaking bitterly.

But honestly,
your rejection of me
has allowed me to see who you really are.
You are bitter,
broken,
and emotionally scarred.

You guard your heart
to cover for the things that you lack.
You are missing class,
common sense,
and tact.
Yes, it's a fact
that I am a flawed woman with character.
But you are looking
for an applauded caricature,
airbrushed falsehoods
you've accepted as truth over time.
It would blow your mind
if you knew that supermodels
don't wake up looking that fine.
Even if you got what you wanted,
would you truly be ready?
You can't guide a relationship
if your captain's hand ain't steady.
And even if the type of perfection
that you wanted did exist,
I doubt she would lower herself
to deal with your...

I know what I'm worth.
Pretend if you must,
but I know that you noticed
my beauty first.
What resides here is the kind of love
that changes the course
of your life forever.
Anything that you do,
my nurturing makes you better.
Royal in the way that I walk.
Wise in the way that I talk.

I'm so bad,
I can peak your desire
without having to take
any of my clothes off.
But you'd rather front and scoff.
I don't care if you're not ready
to accept this truth.
You're so busy trying to cut me,
you don't realize that you're killing you.

But it's cool.
I've taken up enough of your day.
I'll just grab my cookies
and be on my way.
No further words are needed,
so just leave me alone.
It doesn't matter anyway,
right?
I'm just the fat girl in the cookie aisle
whose man is waiting
for her to get home.

# In Defiance

I won't apologize for it.
For my candor
or my strength.
For my wisdom
or my weakness.
For my heart
or my selfishness.
For my needs,
my wants,
my desires,
or my dreams.
For my senses being open.
For my femininity.
For all the things
that tie me to my natural life
and deepen my spiritual being.
They are all uniquely me,
and I won't apologize for it.

# She Is Art

inspired by the "Spiritual Ballerina"

I see the world in rhythm and time.
I feel its pulse under my feet
and I must dance.
I dance until my soul sings
and my lips follow their impulse.
I sing the song of a queen misplaced,
then quietly sit to pen her grace
in written psalms.

# Black Girl Magic

Inspired by a picture taken by Amira Inspired Photography

The heartbeat of African drums
blended with the soul of Renaissance jazz,
composed with Joplin's complexity,
and fused with Gospel's healing power.
Beautiful without parallel,
in every shade of melanin
and lovely curve.
Feminine being born
to nurture and cherish,
to support and inspire,
to love and be loved.
Yeah. That's her.

# More

I am more than a woman.
I am more than the being
that you admire externally.
More than the ability
to think on a surface level;
I'm destined to live eternally.
More than the sway of my hips
as I walk past.
More than the sweet smell
that lingers
or the impression that lasts.
More than you can ever imagine.

I am more than a person.
I am destined to fill shoes,
answer questions,
change lives,
heal hearts
and cure blues.
More than the limitations
placed on me by circumstances.
I keep rising forward.
I take my chances.
I am more than the
stereotypical view of my peers.
More than the prayer
of one mother,
but the prayers of mothers
throughout the years.
More than one set of feet.
More than one set of hands.

Quite possibly,
more than you can ever
understand.

I am more than one minute.
I'm a lifetime of events
for which each second of my life
was meant.
More than the worries
that keep me up at night.
More than the tears.
More than the strife.
More than the skeletons
that fill my closet;
one day, I'll release them
as I should.
More than the wishes of those
who would rather see me fail
than do good.
I am more than one error,
because I can rise above it.
I have only one life.
It's mine.
I'll love it
until God pulls His Breath
from this earthly case.
It is only then that I will be no more
than skin, bones and veins.

But while I am here,
I will exceed expectations.
'No' is not an option.
I am even more than
the dreams and aspirations

that I have for myself.
More than physical beauty
or material wealth.
I can say that I've dealt
with what has been given to me,
but this world is not dealing
with just me only.
The Spirit that resides inside
gives me the drive
to make more than a one-time effort
to say that I tried.
I'm filled with pride,
more than you see on the outside.
If someone told you otherwise,
they lied.

I am more than everything
and yet nothing at all.
I'm strong enough to rise,
yet I'm not too proud to fall.
I am daughter,
mother,
sister,
and friend.
Time and time again,
I will prove that
no man's visions can encompass
what I'm here for.
I am purpose.
I am woman,
and still so much more.

# Lessons

I've learned that there are some things
that shouldn't be believed.

I've learned that understanding
ain't always what you receive.

I've learned that love and life
don't always coincide.

I've learned that some emotions
are impossible to hide.

I've learned that what you want
ain't always what you get.

I've learned that your actions
lead to rejoicing or regret.

I've learned that changes
are always sure to come.

Most of all,
I've learned when the changes stop,
that means you're done.

# For Women

With grace and style.
With elegance and patience.
With beauty and nurturing.
With selflessness and heart.
With resilience and wisdom
passed down through generations.
Withstanding all, we live.
Withholding nothing, we give.
We embody what love means.
We are women.

# IV

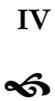

Five to make you smile.
Seven to cause reflection.
Five, seven. five. Done.

(haiku)

# Phoenix

Fall, now get back up.
Past, like ashes, fades away.
Phoenix, rise again.

# Adulting

Can I stay in bed?
Watch cartoons and eat candy?
Nope, because I'm grown.

# Youth

Life gets hard sometimes.
For now, laugh, play and enjoy.
Be the child you are.

# Royalty

I been royalty.
My Daddy's the King of Kings.
What? You didn't know?

# So You Know

You blame it on me.
Seems to be the way these days.
I ain't here for it.

# Assisted Game

Let me help you out.
I see you staring at me.
Call me sometime, K?

# The Answer Is

an acrostic haiku

You asked, "Would our love
extend to eternity?"
So, here's your answer…

# Doors

In life, there's this truth:
Wherever there are closed doors,
there are open ones.

# Manifestation

Your words have power.
God-given authority.
Speak and it is so.

# V

We stay foolishly silent,
for these are the conversations
that pierce the soul.

# When Tired Gets Tired

I feel like it's the eighth day
of the week.
My twist out ain't working,
I've burned my biscuits,
and the tea that I've been sipping
is cold.
I've lost motivation to do basic things
like sewing this hole in my bathrobe.
And I know that it is
unladylike to say this.
I don't care.
Let the neighbors stare
at my unshaped afro.
I left the window open on purpose
'cuz I need some air.
I'm frustrated.
I've been waiting for answers
to questions that I never posed;
but since they affect me,
I suppose I'll wait.
And I've been waiting
and waiting
and waiting
for a response or a hint
that it will all be better soon.
Not trying to be rude,
but we've been waiting for
'soon'
for a long time.
Some gave up waiting.
Some lost their minds.

Some tried too hard.
Some let their spirit die.
Some ain't woke yet,
but once they are,
I'm willing to bet
that they will be given
the same answer –
wait.
In the meantime, they say:
"Get a good paying job.
Be a productive member of society.
Maintain your calm and sobriety.
Deal with your issues quietly.
Stand up but don't stand out.
Help keep our status quo and clout.
If we break your back, don't shout.
Heal quickly and figure it out.
And in all this,
your breakthrough is coming
soon."
I'm getting too old to assume
that 'soon' will come in my lifetime
if I don't make it.
Few chances are given.
Sometimes, you gotta take it.
And I will.
Right now, I can't fake it.
I need to rest.
I've been giving my best
to those that didn't deserve it.
Now I must pause,
reflect,
get nourished,
and figure out

if it's still worth it.
I know it is.
But right now,
I'm just not in the mood.
'Cuz I feel like it's the eighth day
of the week.
My twist out ain't working,
and I've lost that fire.
Yep.
I'm just tired.

# Private Lies

White lies.
Little lies.
Black lies.
Painful lies.
Stories of private lives.
Life lies.
Private lies.

Cherished lies.
Old lies.
New lies.
Bold lies.
Closets of private dreams,
but nothing's ever as it seems.

Quiet lies.
Public lies.
Lies to protect or despise.
Lies to cover business done.
Lies no matter who they're from.

True lies.
False lies.
Misunderstanding of personal cries.
Untold stories of private lives.
Life lies.
Private lies.

# Hashtag

#whatdoIsaytoyou

I guess I can start
with how I met your father.
He wasn't my type.
I was bitter inside
and didn't want to be bothered.
But persistence pays off.
His chivalry soon showed me
that first impressions are misleading.
It wasn't long before
I heard God's voice whispering,
"Daughter, it's him you're needing."
I was hooked,
gone,
singing old school love songs
and dreaming of dresses in white.
I prayed that it was God's will
for me to be his wife.
I was right.
Side by side, I promised all of me
for the rest of my life…

…but wait,
I gotta make it social media official:
#Issawife

It wasn't long before
sweet nights together
brought us our first child.
I had swollen toes and a sour temper,

but he always took care of my needs.
Only God knows how patient
that man was with me.
Well, I was carrying his seed.
After nights of interceding for me,
you were born –
a healthy, beautiful baby girl.
You were a precious gem
born into this world
with purpose unknown
and a dream in your eyes.
Truly, you were mommy's joy
and daddy's pride…

…but before I forget,
let me snap a pic for my followers:
#prettiestgirlalive

I knew that you were a genius
by the age of five.
It was my mission to feed your spirit
and educate you beyond
what you learn
within your school's walls.
I wanted you to marvel
at your melanin
as your natural crown
made you stand tall
despite your short stature.
Daily, I see that God allowed
the best of your father and me
to mix with perfection
and create the blessing

that you were born to be.
Unlimited is your destiny…

…until you start seeing the hashtags
and begin to ask questions.
"Mommy, what does this mean?"

Now, I'm stuck.
I'm unsure of how
to explain this to you.
In some places,
they will not celebrate you.
How do I state the truth?
Melanin means maturity
and cuts short the childhood
of some of your peers?
I wish I could stop the tears
that flowed freely as you said,
"Mommy, they look just like me."
They do, baby.
It's true.
As a mother,
keeping you covered in prayers
is all I can do.
Your father can protect you
and arm you with knowledge,
wisdom,
and wealth.
And we both will teach you
to protect yourself.

But how?
How can I explain to you
that this world ain't fair?

It may judge you based on
the texture of your hair.
How do I say
that your choice of toy
may cost you your life?
How do I say
that candy and sweat tea
might be your last meal at night?
How do I justify
beatings for selling CDs?
How can I explain
that you may be murdered
in the place where you hold the keys?
No, you can't stare too hard.
No, you can't run away.
And a declaration of your rights
might be the last words that you say.

Add your gender and the ante is higher.
Don't play by the rules
in the boys' club?
You're fired.
If you save yourself, you're crazy.
If you slip up once, you're a ho.
You might lose your life
if you make the choice to say no.
Despite it all,
I'm raising you to be a woman of worth.
I want you to be loving,
forgiving,
and true to yourself first.
No, this world isn't all hard.
In the darkest sky,
you can see the brightest stars.

So shine bright, baby.
Cry if you must.
Never give up your fight.
And never,
ever,
ever dim your light.

Still,
I can't hold you forever.
I can't promise that this world
will somehow get it together.
Maybe it will.
Maybe never.
Even in my clever words,
I am speechless.
I owe you reason for this devastation,
though I didn't create it.

So, social media, I turn to you.
Maybe if we come together,
we can get through.
Or at least find a solution
or two.
But until then…

# Quarters

Give me a quarter, pretty lady.
I ain't ate in a while
and I need food to keep on living.

Give me a quarter, pretty lady.
The laundromat cost that much
to wash my shirt.
It's the only one I got, you know.

Give me a quarter, pretty lady.
I can shine your shoes for you.
You can't get that big promotion
without pretty, shiny shoes.

I see you every day, pretty lady,
and I know that you can help me.
Most people pass me by,
ignore or reject me.
They don't know that my situation
doesn't reflect all of me.
I'm flesh and blood like them.
I can tell that your spirit is different.
Please don't disappoint me.

My survival hinges
on these few minutes of your day.
Give me a quarter, pretty lady,
and I'll be on my way.

# Intervention

Folks are out here hurting.
They're desperately searching
for resolution to life's pollution,
some of which they didn't cause.
They're serving heavy sentences
with no clause,
leaving no time to pause.
They want out.
No second guessing.
No chance to get it right.
No time to doubt.
They say,
"Just give me a remedy for this tragedy.
I fought with all that's in me.
Now, I'm ready for this pain to cease.
Give me release."
Those who remain
live with tear-stained pillows
since their family unit has been
decreased.
Painful questions remain unanswered.
"What could I have done better?
Did I love enough?
Was I not present?
Was my criticism too rough?
Did I operate in true empathy?"
Gathered friends and family
are left to piece together
the fragments of their broken souls.
They'll never know how deeply
you felt that hole.

But what if you could hold on
just one
more
day?
You could feel sunrays kiss your skin
or appreciate the coolness
of a summer rain.
Whatever it is,
come what may,
we can face it together.
I can't promise you perfect weather,
but with each morning
comes another chance to see God's glory.
As time goes on,
we can find an alternate ending
to your story.
Folks are out here hurting.
They're desperately searching
for resolution to life's pollution.
If we keep trying,
keep loving,
we may find another solution.

# The Blame Game

I don't know where to place the blame.

Is it on me for allowing
this to commence?
Use common sense, they say.
So am I to blame
for letting you run game
when my heart no longer
wanted to play?
Am I at fault for teasing you
with my natural curves?
Was what I was given at birth
the reason you felt forced to stay?
Did I say the right words
to awaken your manhood
to the point
where 'no' was not an option?
Bottle popping,
talking non-stop.
I thought you were hot,
but my mindset is far
from that line of thought
so I declined.
Was I wrong to still
allow you to touch my behind
as that slow jam played?
Was it my fault
for not walking away?
Or should I have
never came in the first place?

I heard you're the type
that moves at a face pace,
but my soul wasn't ready
for what your body craved.
My mind weighed the options.
To you, there was no stopping.
You used all your best lines.
It was decision time
and you don't hear 'No' often.
How dare that be my answer,
right?
Rage filled your veins
as that gentleman persona
resorted to ravenous behavior.
I screamed for a savior,
but there was no one
to hear my voice.
You stole my choice
with the comfort of knowing
that all you had to say was
'I wanted it'.
You bragged to your friends.
I was your conquest
and you flaunted it.
I became
an unwilling muted seductress,
left to wear the shame
like a tattered dress.
And I guess it was my fault.
They say it's my fault.
Still,
I don't know where to place the blame.

# Skeletons

for "Freedom"

Do you know why
I don't like being alone?
It all comes back to me.
Every memory is stuck on replay
and I long for the day
that the VCR breaks.
Maybe then, I'll stop rewinding
my mistakes.
Even the glory days are overplayed,
leaving me to wonder
what could've been.
I was born to take the high road,
but I found myself constantly giving in.
Time was wasted
trying to fit into places
too low for me.
Failure and Regret
look like good company
because they come dressed as good times
and ready to party.
When it's time to recover,
they vanish.
Maybe they're tardy,
or they're not coming at all.

Do you know why
I don't like being alone?
It's too quiet
and putting pen to paper

doesn't always give resolve.
Life's math gets harder to solve
and tears won't wash difficulty away.
Being surrounded
with souls seeking solace
hides the malice presented each day.
But still, they stay.
Skeletons don't take vacations.
They're patient.
They'll wait for you to return
so they can remind you of everything
that you refused to learn while hiding.
I'm backsliding,
but I think I'm moving forward.
I'm masking avoidance
as handling my business.
Truth is,
I can't move on
until old debts are settled.
Running is easy if the ground is level.
What happens when the road
gets bumpy?
My pace slows to a trot
until I'm forced to stop
because the pain
is not worth the destination
I'm running to.
I still end up cut and bruised.
Bloody shoes
match the bloody hands
that I'm forced to face

as I stand
in front of the skeletons
that demand answers.

Instead of marrying my purpose,
I became life's mistress.
I accepted second best
because what God wanted
seemed too hard.
How can He be a loving God
if doing what's right
still left me scarred?
He said,
"It's for your good."
It seemed like simple common sense.
Impatience turned simple to complex
and I haven't been right since.
Now I sleep with the lights on,
scared that my past will come
to haunt me.
Skeletons chant endlessly to taunt me
as a reminder
of the things that I've done.
I spend nights filled with insomnia,
looking at others' lives thinking,
'I could've been the one'.
Purging and prayer
will only get me so far
if I refuse to leave the burdens
at God's feet.
I've carried them so long
that they are a comfort to me.
Past lives wrapping around me
like an afghan laced in anthrax,

loaded with tainted facts
that both comfort and kill me
slowly.
And it's me only.
The company I kept then
had no desire to be around
when the real battle began.

So here I am again,
fighting for my right to breathe.
I'm desperately searching
for something that I can believe.
Tell me that
changes bring new chances.
Tell me that falls can still fuel.
Tell me that dreams never diminish
and if I am breathing,
there will be something new.
There's no such thing as loss;
either you win or you learn.
And now,
I must cross the bridges
that I've burned.
I'll do it
if it means I can release.
I'll push through it
if I can finally get peace
and tell the voices
reminding me of all my wrongs
to cease.

Do you know why
I don't like being alone?
The world can be so busy

yet simultaneously still.
It will try to break you
for walking in His will.
With each mistake you make,
regret fills your head
and tries to make you feel
worthless.
Your skeletons know your worth
and will try to undermine
the purpose that you were born for.
I know this now.
My skeletons are a part of me,
but not all of me.
I'm not afraid anymore.

# Humanity

The sun rises another day.
Your heart beats like a metronome.
The body prepares to leave the home;
the mind stays in slumber's place.

It's time to join the fray.
You push for family or survival alone.
Wanderlust grows, mind tends to roam
to a calm and peaceful space.

Familiar senses on replay:
corporate conversations and homeless groans.
Loud city noises drown out ringtones
as elusive dollars you chase.

Fatigue is cliché.
Though the future is unknown,
you're thankful for the seeds you've sown.
It's the plight of the human race.

# A Call To Get Up

it can happen if we start today…

He was a young man
with so many dreams
and potential bursting at the seams.
It seems that world wasn't ready.
I guess that's why the force
was deadly.

She was a young girl
with so much purpose,
but she was told her life
was void and worthless.
She was penalized for her hips and thighs.
She never realized that she is the prize.

Stories we see every day,
but we try to turn and look the other way.
We just say that we'll pray.
But who will stay to tell these jewels
the things they need
to learn about themselves,
their real truth?

Truth is they're royalty,
children of light,
and born to lead.
They are the answered prayers
of those before
with history long before these shores.
Their sun-kissed melanin is blessed

and strong enough to pass each test.
They are wise
with so much room to grow.

But if we don't teach them,
they'll never know.

Who will see,
plant the seed,
and fill the need
just so they can reach their destiny?
Or are we content to see
our mother's tears in crimson pools?
If our lives matter,
then this change is overdue.

But who will sacrifice the time?
Who will feed the soul
and free the mind?
There is lots of work to do,
but it simply starts
with you.

# Awakening

An awakening is taking place.
It is starting with the individual soul
reclaiming its right to write
and make whole the heart
of the collective.
It reaches for the rejected.
It calls to all affected,
blinded,
and misguided,
simply saying,
"Wake up."

# VI

Foolishly, this world told me
that my race was not worth running.
They didn't know that God gave me
wings to fly.

# Be Still

So many questions
and opinions of where to go.
There's the lure of possibility
and the fear of the unknown.
I'm at a crossroad knowing
that the choice is mine to fill.
Yet, I hear Him whispering,
"Be still."

There's comfort of returning
to what lies in the past:
the pain, loss, joy and success
that simply did not last.
Newness holds discomfort,
and what's old has lost its thrill.
Yet, I hear Him whispering,
"Be still."

Both roads hold tests and trials.
Both roads require fight.
One is meant to break me down;
one increases my light.
I do not know which road is soft
or which is harder to till.
Yet, I hear Him whispering,
"Be still."

He said, "I'll go before you
to prepare the way you take.
And though you'll stumble, fall and fail,
your spirit will not break.

I know you're anxious to move on;
patience is a bitter pill.
For now, I'm simply asking
to be still."

So I sit at the crossroad
not knowing what's to be.
I only trust that what's to come
is what's best for me.
Until I'm clear on what to do,
I'll stay within His will.
I'll wait on His direction
and be still.

# Joy

Regardless of the circumstance,
still choose joy.
It is the melody
to which your life's song
is written.
It is composed beautifully
with highs and lows,
but it only becomes a
true masterpiece
when you sing it.

# Chasing Shadows

Ain't your feet getting tired
of chasing after shadows?
Reality is right in front of you.
It's tangible,
yet you willingly choose
to run after what is not meant
to be caught.
Do better you ought,
but the unattainable has its appeal.
You run faster,
trying to master movement
on a wheel.
Be still.
Watch the earth move for you.
Catch your breath
as what is yours moves
toward you.
Light shifts the shadows
to be behind you
so you can stop chasing
and find you.

# Dawn

The same Spirit that was present
at the earth's foundation
dwells in me.
It beckons me to my destiny.
And honestly,
you'd think it would be simple.
With the breath of life,
He gives the vision.
Dreams were born
while eyes were closed.
Potential waited to greet the morning
and eagerly anticipated
the sunlight pouring through the window.
But sometimes, dreams remain dormant.
Instead of claiming my prize,
I stayed asleep
and missed the call to rise.

I surrounded myself with souls
wandering in the night,
hoping one of them would teach me
how to find the light
(or at least how to not be afraid of the dark).
The blind can't lead the blind.
It wasn't long before
self-esteem became a lost art,
and every negative word
was taken to heart.
My dream became a nightmare.
Those same wandering souls
tortured my temple without care.

Endless nights
were spent constantly crying
as my God-given light was dimming…

…but never dying.

Every night must have a day,
and the light of the sun
began to boldly shine through.
I began to seek the truth in a new dawn.
You reminded me
that though my eyes could not see,
You never left me alone.
You removed the scales
so I could see the sun
and You could guide me on.
You lifted me to the mountain
that I was born to claim.
Without You,
I would have forgotten
that each valley experience must end.
Rain brings newness for life to begin.
And in all this,
You still call me friend.

The same Spirit that was present
at the earth's foundation
dwells in me.
It beckons me to my destiny.
And honestly,
you'd think that it would be simple.
Despite the flawed nature
of this existence,
the darkness will always give way

to the dawn.
No matter how hard it gets,
I will always thirst for more.
With Him,
something beautiful is always in store
once it's morning.

# On-Time God

The preacher-man says,
"He's an on-time God."

My momma says,
"Stay on your knees and pray."

My daddy says,
"He's your steel and rod."

My granny says,
"He'll wipe tears away."

The old saints say,
"Always believe!"

And in my life, I found
the on-time God
that I perceive
is my peace and solid ground.

# Stones

for those who feel voiceless

I have nothing left to give You.
I am nothing here to note.
I am here at Your feet wondering
if You can restore hope.
I want nothing more than to live free
of the cards I've been given to play.
So God, if You can hear me,
please take these stones away.

They say that I'm the least of all;
You say that's who You love.
They say that You only
watch children and fools.
Well, if I'm Your child
and foolish I've been,
You must be watching me too.

I have nothing left to offer.
I'm broken with no beauty to declare.
But if all are sinners,
are the stones that they've thrown
even fair?
Please tell me You care.

I'm not worth the effort,
or so I've been told.
Can You really make what's common
shine like pure gold?
If so,

here I am.
Please consider me Yours to mold.

I have nothing left to give You
I have nothing more to say.
But if You hear me,
see me,
or love me at all
please take these stones away.

# Rainbows

His promise after the flood

As long as there are rainbows,
      You won't drown in the rain.
As long as there are rainbows,
      There'll be relief for your pain.
As long as there are rainbows,
      You'll have strength to carry on.
As long as there are rainbows,
      I'll hold you up and make you strong.
As long as there are rainbows,
      You'll have hope and peace from Me.
As long as there are rainbows,
      You'll have sweet serenity.
As long as there are rainbows,
      You can hold My Unchanging Hand.
As long as there are rainbows,
      I will give you strength to stand.

# The Gift

I guess you can call me spoiled.
Each morning,
I wake up to a new present.
It is a beautiful gift
given to me by my Father,
the King of Kings.
He wraps it perfectly
in an imperfect vessel.
It's simplistic;
yet with no bells and whistles,
it is the most beautiful,
powerful,
and amazing gift that I could get –
breath.

# Inspired By A Tree

There are no leaves to adorn you,
no wind blowing through you,
nor are there flowers to glorify
the majesty you possess.
But amongst the others
with leaves and blossoms,
you stand tall.

Are you not blooming
due to something you've done,
or is it not your time to shine
and show the world your colors?

I'm sure you're lonely.
You may be feeling neglected.
No one will look at you
and see the beauty you exude.
But amongst the others
with ornamentation,
You stand tall.

If you ever doubt
that you are God's creation,
know that you still reach for the heavens.
You are without question
a testament to God's affection.
And you too will bloom.

# Wings To Fly

a letter to my younger self

As you grow and learn, you'll see
some folks aren't what they said they'd be.
Don't let them steal your destiny.
They'll come around,
they'll sit a spell,
and they'll pretend to wish you well.
They only want to see you fail.
Beware of those who give you praise.
They'll laugh and lie right to your face.
They only want to take your place in this race.
You see,
they think that if they clip your wings,
you'll fall apart right at the seams
and forget all your hopes and dreams.
Ain't that mean?
But they don't know
the God that you serve
embedded purpose from your birth.
You're born to change this very earth.
Know your worth.
Know that what they say and do
will never be the end of you.
Like the phoenix,
rise from ashes strong and true.
And know that you
should never be scared to try,
because you were born
with wings to fly.

# Introspection

When you are alone,
you learn some things about
yourself.
As you search your heart
and cleanse your soul,
you'll find the need for God
to mend the holes.
Tears will flow.
Pain will come.
In His time,
all the wounds will heal.
And you'll smile.
And you'll laugh.
And you'll be yourself
again.

# The Blessing

May your family always prosper.
May all that you touch be blessed.
May your presence equate favor
and bring others success.
And if the sun's not shining,
may you find the light within.
May God bless and keep you.
Ashe and Ashe again!

May all that's been stolen be replenished.
May all that's lost be found.
May the steps you take and moves you make
lead you to higher ground.
May every battle be your victory
and every trial come to a swift end.
May God bless and keep you.
Ashe and Ashe again!

CPSIA information can be obtained
at www.ICGtesting.com
Printed in the USA
LVHW011105300821
696398LV00012B/1388

9 780692 107041